CARAVAN

CARAVAN

Ethna McKiernan

for Gayle
with history and much
admiration —

Ethna McKiernan

Midwest Villages & Voices
Minneapolis

The Dedalus Press
Dublin

Thanks to all who provided generous editorial and other assistance in the preparation of this book; to Anita White and Elaine Pelosini for their art work; to my family, for their support; and to Lynn, Greg, and Pat for years of belief.

Acknowledgement is made to the following magazines and anthologies, in which some of these poems appeared: *Cyphers, Fallout, An Gael, The Lake Street Review, Milkweed Chronicle, The Minnesota Daily, New North Artscape, Northern Lit Quarterly, Northern Sun News, Poetry Ireland, Sanctuary, Si!, Santa Barbara Independent, This Sporting Life* (Milkweed Editions), and *Unlacing: Ten Irish-American Women Poets* (Fireweed Press).

Midwest Villages & Voices
3220 Tenth Avenue South
Minneapolis, Minnesota 55407

The Dedalus Press
24 The Heath
Cypress Downs
Dublin 6, Ireland

for Jeannette and Eóin

CONTENTS

IV THE UNIVERSE STILL STREAMING SUN

CARAVAN

MUSE IN THE MIRROR

Sister, you live in the glass,
my other, outer half
who is a creature all her own
and yet who seems a perfect twin.

Your home is water, light,
or any mirror in the eye
whose clear, unwavering honesty
belies an incapacity for depth.
We are each other's echoes, you and I.

Tonight the lake collects the light,
and every liquid cell
contains an image
wrung from centuries
of looking for the double.

Hands bent to the water,
I see you held still as breath
in its long arms. One finger touch
and you are two, you are four,
split to dozens and as multiple as atoms.

Of those that float to shore,
which am I?

HIGH SCHOOL GIRLS

They think the world is round,
that it revolves around the high school steps,
that a June wedding would be best.

Every morning they arrive
to make a fresh debut, a chorus line
of glazed pastels on board the bus.

From where I sit behind the wheel, their voices rise
and drift like wind chimes—clear glass chords
sustaining insubstantial notes.

We lumber on through early traffic,
bruised and sprung amidst the bumps
of patched spring roads.

No matter: they are oblivious of all of this,
lost in thoughts of last night's date,
or else, perhaps, the going rate for dope.

Through the rear view mirror
I see shreds of aging dandelions
float in to settle in their hair, and

it makes me want to take the corners hard,
to tell them—if they knew—
that every breath they shed

was an investment.
Later, when the fabric of their lives
begins to alter,

hard facts will close them in:
grey hairs and babies will claim them,
and I will open the bus door to their children.

ONE SUMMER'S LAKE

for Lynn Foussard

This is no lake,
it's a flat blue egg. We peel
its shell and climb inside
like four spoons looking for the yolk.

Or else it is a mirror,
giving us only half the truth.
We'll dive for the rest,
cutting the bevel sideways
with a slice.

What surrounds us now?
The moon is a crazy rustler,
rounding up the news.
Water-echoes bounce us remnants,
all the daily gossip.

And now we rise, four
alabaster bodies playing statues.
You are a tropical bird,
grave and lovely,
lifting a wing to the sky.

You say: look, the moon
is a stained-glass belly,
a pregnant melon. Tonight
it will drop an infant moon
for each of us.

Nobody speaks. Your laugh
swims back to shore.

BIOGRAPHICAL NOTES

Described once as the mother of none
caught me flat; as if I were that, and only that.
I think I blustered, "No—yes—but—wait,
aunt of 23, sister of nine, wife of one,"
etc., etc., before I could help myself.

Suppose I were a stone: no pedigree,
total anonymity. Unless centuries of history
burned their mark on me and so bore claim
of some legitimacy
in the definition of that stone.

Not being stone, mornings
I just brush my hair and check the sky
for news of who I am,
what liner notes to sum me up today.
An ordinary woman with no children,

I eat cantaloupe and words for breakfast,
and on the bus I read again, this time
weary novels in the sad riders' eyes.
Damn your definitions: what possible
compressed assembly of parts or motion

can distill a pretty kernel representing all?
Evenings, checking the street for strangers,
I unlock the storefront home
and gladly step into my own warm glossary,
shedding layers of a rigid world's hands.

But some nights, some nights, daughter
whom I've never known, poetry descends
right through the leaking roof
and swarms inside my brain
like honey in a golden river,

wild-currented in spring, splashing
smooth, silent stones,
And it is then, only then,
I could tell you
exactly who I am.

HALLOWEEN

for Siobhán

Small ballerina in a fat pink tutu
wears her tiara crooked; hasn't yet learned
the art of carrying a bag of tricks.
Arms open wide to the world's large treat,
she blooms door-to-door
like a little charged shoot of goodness,
trading smiles for sweets she collects,
an act unequalled by the ghouls and Rambos
who demand more than they leave.

How long, child, before
fairy-godmothers' powers disappear
and the strictures of the street
prescribe where and when your feet can walk,
as the night's harsh arms
begin to squeeze?
For the moment you are safe:
in the magic cloak of childhood
you can wander where you please.

Dance, sleeping beauty,
twirl your pale gauzy skirt
until you drop, drowsy on the bed.
Then lie still: let your blonde hair grow
for one hundred years
and the forest thrust forth
cruel brambles elsewhere.
As you dream, your candies pirouette
across the floor like graceful sentries,
watching till you wake.

STILL-LIFE ON INISHEER

from "The Island Poems"

In the low stone houses,
the dream-fires begin to stir.
Somewhere from sleep, an old woman sighs
and laughs for sheer release,
circling back beneath the ice
to greener years.

She does not hear her husband rise
and wind his woollen way
down toward the blue-throated sea,
where his bony curraghs
huddle on the sand
like a pair of hands curved in prayer.

He is a nightwalker:
says he feels some days a strange decay
has settled in upon the island
like an old neighbor coming home to die.
He will fish now in darkness, riding out
where the waters clear themselves of ghosts.

She has made her peace with sleep,
and turns above her pillows
to embrace familiar ghosts,
dreaming the island and she are aged whispers
whittled from an older roar,
with all their edges honed and muted down
till they've become like sand or air.

An ancient moon trembles
and silhouettes the woollen man
in chalky tones.
He lays his wrinkled cheek upon his mounded nets,
and lets himself drift
further and further from home.

CÉILÍ MÓR

from "The Island Poems"

Half daft with music,
flushed with drink,
sweaty as cows at yesterday's market

we spun all night in giddy step
and stamped our neighbors' toes
three inches to the left.

The bank played reels and waltzes
till the breathless crowd had stopped;
the arms around waists were prizes carried off.

And hours afterward, just this—
two bodies in an empty room
still circling in around desire

toward the prize not given yet,
that final dance
into the liquid elegance of sex.

TO INISHMORE

from "The Island Poems"

The boat engines whir and hum
and the gangplank scrapes shut.
Cold sounds, final languages.

Someone is always leaving, leaving—

In Mexico, the child cries to his mother
as the train pulls away, while somewhere else,
perhaps, events and bodies gladly break apart.

Above the ship, gulls are thrashing the air
to bits. Their high calls
slice the air like knives, a Greek chorus.

Did the woman in the black dress there
leaning toward the wind,
fall, last night,

before she closed her eyes,
to that old lie
of softness in dark?

Remote, awkward today,
empty of promises
as the grey Galway sky,

we'll part strangers again,
blank as the creamy surf
that rings the shipsides

as your boat glides out into the distance.

FOREIGNER

from "The Island Poems"

In early moonlight
old men dangle crossed legs
from bleached stone walls
and every turn of air
seems an electric shock,
a ghost with hands.

Further up the path
the only light
is one fluorescent rosary,
discarded plastic
flung upon a fuchsia bush
where now it glows crazily.

On such a night
the Clare coast split
and drifted out to sea;
ground collapsed
and Inis Meáin was born.

But darkness can dissolve the past.
This tarred black sky
absolves all secrets, any ancient sins.
Thick with history,
the bloodstains on the ringed stone fort

clot quietly till dawn,
then fade to vaguest rust
with sun.
Panic lies in silences like this,
and this is no country for strangers—

where the faint click of lights
going down on the next island,
and even the harmless
greasy breakfast eggs
ejaculate a menace of imperatives,

the urgent posting
of boat schedules
in an unknown tongue.

ALL TOGETHER NOW

OK, friends, I'll ask my selves
just how it was we came to this:

Before—believe me, I sang
beneath the willows in the kind emperor's court
in China, the year before I fell from grace
for making silver sounds that unbound women's feet;
a mystery to me. For this I was exiled,
and though centuries have kited by, I still see
the emperor awake in the canopied bed, each fluid note
I taught him fretting through his head.

Or the years in France, the grapes
purpling my skin
right through to cells in fingertips,
clutch, snip, and a clump in the bucket;
kneeling in mud through rain-crazed days
of raw-handed weariness, till
the sweet crop began its other life
away from earth, pointed wineward
toward American fluorescence, *grand cru* style.

Remember Veracruz! I played marimba
in the Zocalo, and every night whirled by
in panacolor; only the Gringos grey
in pale discussion over black coral
necklaces: How many pesos, Señor?
We plunked the keys and beat the drums
till dawn rose like a new oil field,
gold flames that lit the waves
breaking on the Gulf.

Then here, to the city of wind-chill factors,
where I finally gave it up to the boys of the prairie;
thought seriously about loons and compost heaps,
unlearned dance and poetry; shed my old street life.
Now I flatten daily, thinner than peeled garlic skin,
barely squeaking in
through the stern Scandinavian door.
My personas grow confused (what land is this?)
homesick for song, black dirt, and Mexican waterfront.

I'll tell you friend, this time I'm determined
to conform: punch the clock and hear alarms,
visit the animals on the farm. And if the last
schizophrenic one of me refuses to be tamed, the one
who yearns to hitch-hike back to the Pacific,
then I say let's throw her on a raft
to the wild muskies in Lake Harriet.
When we meet again, integration
and stability just might set in,

and those other transients I own
can hop the next train south.
Then all the sisters, brothers of my separate selves
who bear the marks of older scattered lives
in foreign parts will bow before the mayor
and be granted permanent asylum.
We'll take the oath with one lid closed:
we're here to stay, as one,
or two. . .or three. . .no promises given; just maybe.

DEAR FRIEND

I have written this so many hundreds of times:
"Dear Friend, Dear Friend, Dear Friend,"
litanies of brush strokes
across the white snow of paper, years of silence
sleeping on the page.

To begin now is to start in the middle
of a train journey across the continent,
when the cast of passengers has already changed twice
and each new border
brings a switch to different languages.

If my pen could paint, absent one,
this is the picture I'd send to the country
where you live: white margins
for the frozen breeze that blows after funerals;
black varnish for words that choke in throats

and stop; green tendrils, blue swirls for stalks
that rise beside the tracks despite old lives,
and at the center of the canvas, a red mouth
glimpsed through the train window,
still searching for the voice to speak.

CLIFFS OF FALL

O the mind, mind has mountains; cliffs of fall...

Gerard Manley Hopkins

Elaine Pelosini, © 1989

FIRE

Years ago at 5:00 a.m. I saw the city on fire,
pink glass buildings blazing in the mirror behind.
The river was charged with light, flame fragments
leaping up in orange licks, the water spitting heat.
Two hours later it disappeared; flat grey descended,
and manic visions slithered back beneath the bed.

Yet that queer incongruity
of flame and water paired together still whispers
through my veins the name of something beautiful.
The magnetic field I live in switches into high flux
and I'm at the edge again in seconds,
poised in diving costume for the jump.

Fire: I've lived it, died it, raced like electrons
alongside it, hidden in the cold heart of snow banks
to avoid it. Right now my brain's as hot as it can get.
One match, and I'd burn in hell readily
for the brief joy of watching flicks of light build
from sizzle into roar as they explode against the sky.

MORNING REVELATIONS FROM THE COSMOS

I know what the black wires mean
against the pale fire sky
with one bird astride the wires
precisely where they verge.

I know, too, that the frail garden parsley
must endure its placement
near the chalk-bone blue of broccoli
the worms have chewed.

All this knowing makes my backbone sway
a bit, and the ground somewhat unsteady;
like opening the lid to the world's great core
and breathing the power that smolders there.

But God must choose the chosen
carefully, and so he tests the depths of wisdom
coursing through my blood, hurling out
tongues of riddles, faster and faster

they babble from grooves in tree bark,
buzz and swoop through hidden airwaves
of the morning, chatter slyly
from the very blades of grass underfoot.

But I know. I know
each foreign word, each holy note
the one black bird whistles from his perch
upon the wires up above. I know. I know.

WHAT WE CANNOT HELP

In the evening bridge reflections,
buses seem to travel underwater.
Their headlights span a path among the fishes,
while inside, the drowned riders sleep peacefully,
their hair streaming from the windows
like seaweed, dreaming.

And the streetlights, too, discard their twins
into the river, halves in search of other halves,
an ancient cellular memory.
And it is such seductive kindness—
that warm light which could be candles
holds the frozen dead beneath its surface.

But see the bus conductor now:
so tenderly he monitors the volume
of the sinking passengers' songs,
tape-recording each small gurgle,
saving here a bracelet, there a shoe,
icons of the little river shrine he hopes to build.

And every night he makes this run,
captain catching those who long ago lost track,
as he looks backward to his own past
for that small boy
who promised he'd emerge some time
into the hurt of daylight

with poems, a rocking horse,
kept promises
and no more midnight sailings.
But tonight the underwater bus
will journey onward into morning,
cleansing its sad cavity

with tongues of water
speaking every language
of forgiveness.

SPEED

1
Time stampedes through the flowers
minutes to years the petals fall
furiously snow turns, the hours
snatch the last utterance
from some dying throat
and suddenly the infant
pays the mortgage on the house.

There were canals
once
boats had grace.
We were slow
wore our calm like amulets,
knew despair
but simply chose to keep on walking.

Then steam: coal: trains:
sonic boom:
the atom split
and one remote space vessel
blurred and sped above
in regions of unknown ice.
The nightmare had begun.

2
I tell you, there was terror
on that child's face.
I saw him staring, glazed
into the changing fire,
and all his concentrated gaze
was hurtling forward to the grave.

But the girl's white profile,
her white child arm
alive, an arc
calling him back.
Frail, that act of faith.
Tears have fallen for far less.

3
Leaves, light green,
speed to magenta
fall and fly, bare, bare,
two broken trees, snapped clean.

Never to see
those charged trees
the same way again.

How rapidly we leave.

LETTING GO THE WOLVES

I hear the snow crust crack
into spider-fine antenna lines
with every thudded footbeat. It is so still
that their light scratch of nails on ice
rasps the air like flakes of metal filings.

In the cave where I wait
the fire telescopes their distant pelts
into a thousand single-bladed fibers,
each electric silver hair
a life, a weapon of its own.

There is still time to wonder
how their throats look fully open.
Are they sharp foam-white
or soft-tongued membrane pink? Each year
we've danced this ritual dance,

those animals have never tasted more
than the dank smell of terror
the black mind exudes, hanging
palpable in clumps outside the cave.
This time, maybe, flesh.

Now their tails swish and click,
pocking newly fallen snow. Outside
they are sniffing, pawing at the door
and they're no longer patient:
we've been through this before.

So let the fire roar higher
when I at last invite the lupus in,
and grant me any final revelation
as their hard eyes brighten
when the suicide begins.

ELEGY AGAINST THE DYING OF THE LIGHT

for Steve Arhelgar

After shock passes,
grief and anger still remain—
for your bright blond hair
scarred red by blood,

for your talents cut mid-air
hanging slack now, inert—
for gunshot crack
that wasn't accident,

for a grand slam ending,
home-plate harder than the stone
growing by the river flats
where I see you yet—

for the sheer waste of it,
the universe still streaming sun
and you, Mercedes man,
old companion, steady con,

lured by your own laughter
sparking like July 4th fires
gone awry in dark,
you've finally fallen

under, not a tender bone
left nesting
in your shattered head—
damn you, praise you,

friend: I loved you
and you're dead.

THE MORAL ORDER

Half-asleep under the narcotic sun
an image shifts, flashes blue, green,
holds a signal, invitation spurned.
It changes rapidly, though I call
and call to it: *who are you, are you, who, who.*

Now it is my daughter never born,
"Aisling," dream or vision.
And now she is eleven, sure-boned,
all bright nerves primed outward
singing loudly to the world.
At twenty, maybe, she repeats mistakes
another mother'd claim to die to change.

Of course she fades.
But other images replace hers and remain—
this movie reel's too fast
for me to name their names,
except perhaps the butcher
whom I gave my full consent—
looked him in his knowing eyes
and shook his smooth white hand.

Fever, sunburn. I'd choose amnesia
or evasion ten to one instead of this:
a mortal act which cannot be undone,
the unborn daughter's strong melodic name
is letters burned on stone.

Was this what Moses felt?
Learning for the first time awe,
or something greater than himself
he never knew before,
in that image, that immense regret he sensed
rising from those tablets
with their stricken words in stone.

HOSPITAL

The last tray of opaque paper cups
makes its rounds through the ward tonight.
The way our common throats tilt back
and swallow seems a holy act, homage
to those gentle pills and liquids we ingest.

Now twilight steamrolls slowly through the station,
pausing at my neck like the hot breath
of some animal I cannot see.
It is the hour of rest
and unremembered dreams, the long walk

toward the bright noose of sleep,
coiled and patient as a lover
waiting for embrace. Click the night-light off.
I'll go down peacefully, willing as a child
to wrap myself inside this flannel cloud.

WHAT SEASON

It was as if nature's palette
had been stripped overnight
to primal blacks and whites.

Mostly white prevailed,
as when the bright afterimage
of a blooming mushroom shell

was seen forever after
as an imprint on the eyelid
of those who lived to tell.

Or later, in the chalk-bone ash
drilling each ounce of ground
like the final face of hell.

And what shall the infants play
in their stump-armed underworld
centuries from now

when trees have barely
just begun to be again,
and the ceiling of the cellar

darkens year by year,
while tiny balding heads
whiten into winter

that is blacker, crueller
than the ancient word
nuclear.

ARCTIC EXPEDITION

Instead of hands, we held
ropes in human chain
fastened ten feet down the line
to each man's wrist.

When the white-outs came, snow
closed our throats and severed vision
back to camp. Then, we'd wrestle terror
worse than any avalanche.

It's six long months
since the bush pilot dropped us
cleanly to our gear, and the folly
we'd imagined an explorer's glory.

Today his battered Cessna's scheduled to return.
Once home, I'll steel-wool the fungi
off my unwashed chest
and never dream again, please God,

of the moment when the rope slackened
and the first of us was lost to bears,
some said; though I alone carry the load
of a snow-stunned act: the letting go his cord.

MOVING

for Greg

1
Down to the drawers with old string,
marbles, half-burned candles,
a bent childhood photograph.

Now the great bulky past
lies locked in boxes once again,
layered like our years together
and coldly summed up by its labels.

2
There is something frightening
about completely empty rooms—
the white scrubbed walls
cast dim mirror shadows
of all their former occupants

and already
I am flashed up there
among the line-up of those ghosts.

3
Each time I do this
I swear I'll never leave again.
There are pieces of you scattered here
in every box,

like the tiny helicopter flowers
blowing from the maple tree
outside my kitchen window.

And the weight of that luggage,
carrying you around like this,
grows heavier with each move.

4
If it were in my power,
I would kneel before these boxes,
before the honey-wood table
where we once shared food,

beside the photographs
too difficult to divide,
and the record albums all singing
wrong songs from a different era,

and there I would gently light
my brightest matches to that past,
till the room and all its contents
slowly flamed to pink, burning
beautifully and unstoppably
behind me.

5
Unlike Lot's wife,
I would never look back.

THE MUTE ANSWERS BACK

in response to Thomas James' "Letter to a Mute"

You were never alone like this,
pressure-swollen with a language
that no one understood.

As when an instrument
great with urgency of music
vibrates soundless
when overlooked on moving day
and, unheard, ceases song.

Oh, I could tell you stories:
if my tongue had hands
they would build
a multi-lingual castle
where arias would shock the halls

till shards of plaster
burst their spines
and crashed the floor
in unloosed chords
of violent dinful joy.

But it is always evening
on this avenue of statues
and incessant silence,
and tonight the rain I'll never hear
is only soft sensation on my arms,

while I stutter out my impotence
in hoarse unlovely noises,
stumbling and calling you
and calling you again
with every living voice I know,

talking to myself.

LEARNING THE FAMILY

AFTER LOVING

We have no need of speech.
The spirit lives in the skin,
speaks from the pulse in the neck,
glows from finger bones
like a private fire.

Bodies lose their plurality here.
Now we become the smallest atom,
incapable of breakage.
Anything we were fades
to another vision, a past life.

Again and again your face turns to me,
singing shut the distances.
It is more beautiful
than the naked moon.
I will not leave in the morning.

ÅTERKOMST

("Homecoming"—from the Swedish)

We circle the road three times more.
Rings of space, that's all,
where your grandmother's house
once stood—aiways, always,
you'd thought as a child.
Now rusty chunks of farm machines

hurt the ground
where neatly planted fields had grown,
and weeds spike up
like tiny chain saws
gnawing through the soft barn shell.
All that immigrant energy lost! No corn

juts skyward; the animals dead, or migrated.
But look, the Groundhouse River,
and time rears back its neck
to six small bullheads
strung from a boy's old bike,
smacking the air while he pedals home,

alive when doused an hour later
in ice water; Grandmother and you
both giddy with surprise.
Now you cast your lines out again,
reeled back from the planet
of acute childhood lands,

black pole erect
and taut stoic thread strung just so
in perfect cadence to the memory
of an old woman long gone.
Oh, like an anthem
saved in final overture,

you conduct these waters
in bowed grief, raising
fish, corn, soybeans
to a Scandinavian tune,
a song for what's been gained,
a prayer for what's been ruined.

MY MOTHER'S HANDS

I lift the nightgown over my head
but it is my mother's hands I hear instead.
Thirty years back, her fingers are quiet burrs
snagging small rips through the silences
of folded laundry piles, a sandpapery bristle
against old lingerie, softened linens,
even the stiff diapers of the ninth child.

I swore then *my* hands would escape
cream-smooth into adulthood,
not knowing, Mother, how the body
disobeys in time; how skin roughens,
tears and cracks past boundaries of repair,
how at a certain stage these woman's hands
would rasp the same tune on flannel
as your own.

POSTSCRIPT: MY LAI

My daughter is dead.

The flame at the center
no longer burns; the wind wails
lost and broken through the hut.

When it was over,
I wanted to strangle in grief.
They told me peace would come with sleep,

but each time I closed my eyes
I saw her face explode a thousand times
and heard her scream out "Mother."

Now blood chokes the rice paddies,
and only bones float up
to greet the harvest.

My daughter is dead.

WINTER WIDOWER IN KEY WEST

What remains now
in memory
under constant mild sun
is the sheer abandon of it then:

not the bitter days of snow
stiff-casketed
against New England windowsills;
nor the calves' writhings

finally stilled to ghosted forms
like rigid plants
statued white by wind
lassoing drifts under their feet;

not even that blackest winter
that the years won't erase,
when pneumonia seized the child
by degrees, like dropping mercury—

bright petal, paler petal,
brittle curlings on the ground.
Then, Mary, you broke too, just wilted
like the frost-hurt yellow roses

we grieved piece by falling piece
in the aging summer of our last heat,
when afterward, you joined them
underground.

Here, an old man deserves reprieve:
the mindless lap of waves,
noon naps in winter sun,
an afternoon martini in the shade.

But that abandon: oh, when we were young,
we threw ourselves three feet deep
into the snow, making angel arcs
en route to China we believed below.

And we hunted snowflakes by the net,
giddy with hysteria, release,
strong bones triumphant
with that landbound catch,

some heady spininess
to us then, some raw angularity
alien to winter
in Key West.

CATCH

for Russ

I imagine us dancing, a Mexican ballroom somewhere
(anything instead of fishing)
in faded, pre-war elegance, tropically flowered wallpaper
(jigs, flies, speckled lures and mr. twisters)
drooping lushly like the evening sea-breeze
(damn the wind, they won't bite now)
and you in sailor whites—a tuxedo, if I blur my eyes
(black, shiny, slimy leeches, grubs, chubs, fatheads...)
the band plays '40s swing, a dark man croons "Darling"
("I'm a rapid oxidizer," you announce, sweat streaming
        down your nose)
"Darling, Take My heart..."
(walleye, pike, sunstroke, crappies)
and my red dress spins faster as you lift me off the floor
(jesus christ, a four pounder!)
its ruffled hem streaming round my knees
(landed)
like a school of tiny iridescent fish
(darling, take my heart)
you sing at last.

JAZZMOON

And we are so hungry,
full of lust and tears
beneath the full moon

and the saxophone, and the white mist
of heat rising from your coffee cup,
and no light   but piano sparks

on snow, on our childhoods
trembling on the ground in shiny bits
and growing up between us

in the unglued places at our feet.
But the music slides undone,
and this moon won't stop either

it is a full note jarring
in my fullest throat,
a nighttime shudder

spreading silver and betrayal
on the table, on the snow,
on the white moon burning in my bones.

ST. JAMES ORPHAN

*"It was surrounded by enormous high prison-like walls.
Entrance was gained through a great doorway, permanently
closed. It was in this doorway, a century or so ago, that a
little revolving contraption had been inserted into which
mothers placed babies for whom they could no longer care.
By turning it around, they could send the little child into
the awful prospect of almost certain death in the work-
house."*

from *Against the Tide*, Noel Browne

Mother

As if we had a choice.
The three-penny upright on the street
who lifts her tired skirts to faceless men
a dozen times a day
doesn't choose, either; no more
than my body planned to spill out
five weak babies, the lump sum
of my husband's blunt hunger.

I've seen their faces
in the shadows of St. James,
those other mothers parting with young flesh.
If looks could kill, this city'd reek
of death.

You were my smallest one,
little runt among the sparrows,
lame last-born girl.
"Suffer the children," Father Conroy says,
but I don't believe it
any more.

Child

They wake you arguing.
You've heard the words so many times
by now they seem a lullaby:
too many mouths, the bread's run out,
no coal, one boy, three girls,
again another girl.
The song ends like a warped psalm.
And you sleep.

Your mama whispers that it's just a dream,
dresses you in winter knickers,
the Sunday-best grey dress. Her kisses
heat the pre-dawn cold. You sleepwalk
through the Dublin slums
to walls that block the sky of light,

then she lets go your hand.
One world ends
as you watch your mother's face
closing for the last time
while the small shelf
slowly swings you into darkness.

FOR NAOISE UNBORN

First one, little fish,
you kick and dart and glide
beneath my ribs
as if they were your private reef.

For months I've felt you fatten
like a mollusk,
each swell and bump of you
a new pearl.

Sea-newt, limpet-child
I've never known,
I am your mother ocean:
my arms are waves

holding you, I rock
your tiny bones
inside the brine.
Sleep here, you're home.

THE OTHER WOMAN

You visit her house for the first time without him.
She offers you tea, a still-warm jar of raspberry jam,
kindness to trouble your insides.
Later you walk outdoors into the perfect garden,
and it is too clear that the apple trees
have been tended carefully for years,
for they are verging on their first green fruit.
Everything here, in fact, has roots.

Inside now her children fan about her
like blue stones in a peacock's upraised tail,
and every facet of each gem
throws back his reflection, too.
It is too beautiful, too cruel.

At night he comes to you once more
and you are not innocent,
knowing precisely where
to place your hands upon his back
while he breaks his loneliness inside you.

So you hold him, you hold his past, you hold
the faint shadow of his wife
which staggers there between you,
you hold a gift of jam
and an empty, outstretched hand,
awake, thinking of her,
even as she thinks of you.

WEDDING: A DECADE AFTERWARD

In the backward glance, smiles
and the blurred wavings of hands held
in slow motion, permanent photograph.

But say the photograph unfreezes.
Say two people peel forth without context,
unknowing either the world or themselves.

Maybe immigrants! Or pioneers:
the New World to mould, explore and sharpen,
and all their senses primed for that discovery.

Or not. Perhaps just flat and failed
mythologies, resigned
and common as the neighbors' lives.

Then always afterward, a tightening of the heart
at certain moments—in a crowd, say,
or some odd wedding where the flashbulbs click—

reminds them of the camera
that caught, once, and countless times before,
an act of innocence,

and framed it shut
and far away
from change.

THE UNIVERSE STILL STREAMING SUN

STARTING OVER: THE WHITE CANVAS

for Ann Tallentire

Typed pages, fickle as autumn leaves
spiralling from the attic eve. Gone—
a plane landing mid-Atlantic, divers fishing
manuscripts, perplexed, muttering Greek.

Let lake and algae take them now, green the words
into bleached oblivion, nothingness
beyond clear water rounding stones
or drowning swords; the zen of letting go.

And sprinkle, spray them on the grounds,
those tiny alphabets of sound, drizzle them
on crumlins: they'll never be as strong
as my private cache of spiders

webbing threads between these chimney towers,
fierce delirious nets
far more tensile, delicate
than minute scrawlings drifting down.

Goodbye, Monaghan,
and kindly Sir Tyrone,
just for this moment
it's possible I'm found.

at the Tyrone Guthrie Arts Centre
Annaghmakerrig, Co. Monaghan
Ireland

GOING BACK

Here: it must be where you stood,
one hand raised to shade your eyes
against the harsh Atlantic
grinding shoulders with the rocks below.

How your skirt cut the wind in half!
And how you waited, brooding
for the boats that stitched their slow way in
with ribbonned wakes a deeper green,
and each new ship
a promise that you couldn't keep.

I see the girl you were
walk back alone to her father's house,
caught between two hungers.
Some absent strain of music kept you restless,
and I know how the longing worked on you,
for even at night
the boats sent out a siren tongue—
foreign to your ear, perhaps, but song.

One day you finally left,
sailing your boat straight into the cave
of America's open arms;
feeling the wind no monster
there, after such lean dreams
as you had culled from Irish soil.

Mama Mór, I stand here now
where you once stood,
the unchanged land beneath my feet,
certain that my bones were formed
from that same air
that made your bones first stir.

But the old heritage breeds a different pain in me:
a stranger to both countries,
I cannot make my roots take hold;
can only stand and hear the sea
return the poems that you'd willed it
as a child, while the wind
raises ghosts behind me.

HIGH DIVER AT THE FAIR

A tiny woman perches 90 feet above the crowd.
Below, the wind is roller-coastering our hearts,
snapping rainbow pennants like electric laundry
round the pool. She concentrates,
standing on a small wedge of faith
large enough for just two feet.
She is Joan of Arc examining the stake,
Frank Lloyd Wright hypnotized by line,
by form, direction; Einstein weighing matters.
Suddenly the slightest braid of muscle
flicks her body forward toward us
like a floodlight, stunning the sky
with its grace and speed. Our raised eyes
cheer, our hands smart applause,
as she enters the water unscathed,
a whistle of lithe air.

AT THE CHIROPRACTOR'S

Maybe in another life
the doctor tuned pianos,
pressing black discordant notes
like knobs in a backbone
cracking into form.

Underneath the creaky lid,
the big-top of piano skin,
she untangles sinews of unruly chords,
pronging each stringed muscle
that I own.

Lighter now, I hardly know
how to wear
this fine-tuned set of ivory bones:
my coat holds in sonatas
swooping spineward down

and I, a new instrument entirely,
I glide upright
out the doctor's door
as a stooped baby grand
lumbers in.

HISTORY OF PROPER NOUNS

at the Vietnam War Memorial, Washington, D.C.

They are so small from here—
John Anderson   Earl Bernhardt   James E. Bates
ankle-high letters on a black marble wall,
the plain annunciation of names
of the first three American dead.

It must have begun as simply as this,
one inch, one foot at a time,
till boots lost track of distance
and fell feet up into months, into years,
into the last blank stare of space.

The wall steepens on the path down
as spotlights brighten thousands more names.
Their letters breed above my head
like a disease: *Michael   Phillip   Robert   Seán*
a litany of lives dwarfed to characters on stone.

And, for an instant, Hades overwhelms
the mild sunlight of a winter's day, surreal
and terrible, as if a dark grenade of language
holding each casket stretched underground
from Maine to Arkansas,

from Oregon to Florida,
had exploded and rained down some mute lexicon
of syllables long since grown cold; as if
Jim Morrison had walked back from the dead, singing
This is the end, my beautiful friend. . . .

A second taper of black marble and the wall stops.
Stepping into daylight, the brisk sky is so blue
it almost bites, and the burnt-gold flowers
lying at the last name   glow
like the aftershock of light at dusk

or the heated glitter in a young man's eyes
open and blind at noon in a jungle forest.

LOVE POEM IN A FOREIGN TENSE

And there we found three round stone forts
on a rock-blown pathway
winding sidely by the River Slaney.

Under the crimson dropping sky
while brittle light still lit the air
before the bright cold moon

could age us once again,
we unbuttoned our adulthoods
and stepped backward into small light garments

we wore centuries before,
joyously amidst the spare, gifted moments
such as this.

And there we found three small ringed forts
built closely to each other
with amazing stones

which chanted "history," "community,"
the simple act of sunrise,
the natural peace of death.

And for an instant we were plural.

And we each stood magically
in a common passageway
to the three children's forts,

made humble by discovery
on the rock-blown pathway
winding sidely by the River Slaney.

And though night comes as all nights must,
and we will slowly step into the present tense
of our centers, the single lonely centers

of our separate cores,
for that instant
we were plural

by the small stone forts
on the rock-blown pathway
winding sidely by the River Slaney.

INSTRUCTION FROM A SELF-MADE MENTOR

The poet told me if I were serious,
I would isolate myself
and eat nothing but almonds
soaked in white wine
for a year and three days.
He said this recipe had certainty,
would bleach the mind
and sharpen it for revelation.

Anyone could sense his gravity:
he offered wisdom
as though it were some precious essence
to hoard through a shortage.
His hair was white
and his eyes were bright,
though somewhat hard.
I knew he'd learned the secrets long ago.

So I readied myself for a vision quest,
solemn and wide-eyed and ripe.
I set up a shrine to Orpheus
and did my incantation daily.
I ate almonds till my tongue was white
and smooth and clean,
like the heart of one, split open.
Then I turned to wine
and purified myself some more.

The poet built his life on this.
Now he drives an El Dorado
and rubs his pockets fondly,
dreaming of the next edition
of messages and myths
for serious young poets.
Last time I saw him, he winked.
I did what I had to do:
I shot him with my .22.

DANCING THE BOYS INTO BED

Crazy with giggles, a knee-high tornado
is dancing my skirt into knots.
His younger brother's slung across my shoulder,
bobbing his head to some infant dream.

They are the princes of Baba
and I am the palace queen
with regal peanut butter on her cheek.
We are kissing the world goodnight,

skimming a child's cha-cha
across the wooden floor, prancing our feet
to the beat of the baby's hiccups
in the bedtime world of Baba.

Sway, boys, rock the giddy room
to bits. I'll blanket down the castle
and toss some stars above your cribs,
then gently dance you into sleep.

HOUSE/LIGHT

Meagre, but delirious with light—
a house lit with gladiolas in a perfect urn,
blossoms floating in a saucer in the bedroom.

Dreaming, I've entered this house before
a dozen times, testing each spring and gleam
of oak floor for permanence; the high-set windows

for possibilities of truth they may disclose,
the slant of light for certain angles
that might nurture indoor garden growth.

Yet something in the broad prairie
that these rooms suggest
must be a trick of structure only,

and I still resist believing that I hear
the walls whispering *come in, come in,*
mo chroí; you're home, you're free.

Visiting, I've heard the low flutter
of a restless bird in the attic, troubled
by her struggle whether she should leave or stay.

Dreams claim these houses are pieces
of our used psyches, buildings we erect
from planks or shingles pried loose

from the sleeping mind's cave,
until they grow themselves
into dwellings we already knew

but couldn't yet recognize awake.
I don't know—some nights
I think I'm growing closer

as I practice small steps forward
toward the leap I want to make—
from primate speech of dreams

into the language that I'd rather speak,
walking syllable by bright syllable
into the house which utters light,

to the man carrying blazing flowers,
house, house, light, light,
the heavy dove of harmony

resting gently on my shoulders,
claws asleep,
at peace.

Ethna Maeve McKiernan was born in New York and moved to Minnesota via Ireland. She holds a Bachelor of Science degree from the University of Minnesota and is a 1989 recipient of a Minnesota State Arts Board grant. She manages the firm of Irish Books and Media in Minneapolis, where she lives with her two sons.